CW00517547

BEST YOUTUBER EVER.